We hope this booklet, together with the introductory talks on DVD, will give you a better understanding of sensitive end-of-life issues. Each section consists of discussion questions, Bible references, quotations and a prayer by Celia Bowring.

The DVDs are presented by John Wyatt, with introductions by Philippa Taylor.

Professor John Wyatt has worked as a consultant neonatologist at University College Hospital for more than twenty years, but is now concentrating on teaching and research into ethical dilemmas raised by advances in technology. He is past Chair of the Medical Study Group of the Christian Medical Fellowship (CMF) and a board member of Biocentre. His book *Matters of Life and Death* is published by IVP.

Philippa Taylor is Head of Public Policy at the Christian Medical Fellowship and is also a Consultant to CARE on bioethics and family issues. She has an MA in Bioethics, and for the past twenty years has been speaking, writing and working on a range of contemporary bioethical issues. She is also a competitive runner.

Celia Bowring is prayer coordinator for CARE and has written the CARE *Prayer Diary* for over thirty years. Married to Lyndon Bowring, Executive Chairman of CARE, she is also a speaker and writer.

Contents

Preface

For many of us, everyday life is often characterised by efforts to stave off the ageing process. Diets, lifestyle, vitamins, exercise, replacement organs - it's a major industry, as Bryan Appleyard points out in his book, *How to live forever or die trying!* And the sociologist Zygmunt Bauman has suggested that this medicalisation of daily life represents the primary strategy of modern times for suppressing the fear of death. For most people, death is a terrifying prospect.

There's no doubt that the Christian community has much to contribute to the theme of death and dying, and it is important that we speak up. Some of the most substantial challenges to the Christian faith today relate to the question of our human identity. On several significant fronts - whether human sexuality, transhumanism, or beginning- and end-of-life issues - the biblical view of humankind needs to be defended, explained and modelled in the public arena. John Wyatt's contribution to the area of medical ethics is well known, and

this study course on death and dying is welcome and timely.

At the same time as the London Olympics, the Keswick Convention ran a three week event on the theme of Going the Distance - living the Christian life in the light of eternity. John Wyatt's compassionate and insightful lecture on the subject of this study guide was an outstanding part of that theme, and is the reason why Keswick Ministries is honoured to support *Finishing Line*, together with CARE.

Dag Hammarskjold once said that no philosophy that cannot make sense of death can make sense of life either. Christians, therefore, have the opportunity, by personal example and compassionate care, to show the world what it means to die well, and therefore to live well. Jim Packer once suggested that the Christian should approach death in the same way as children prepare for a summer holiday - packed up and ready to go, well in advance! This study guide will help us to do that, and help others to do the same.

Jonathan Lamb
CEO and Minister-at-large for Keswick Ministries. Vice President of International Federation of Evangelical Students

Foreword

What a great privilege it is for CARE to have worked alongside Keswick Ministries and Professor John Wyatt to produce this unique resource. It's designed especially for small groups - where Christians can get to know each other enough to discuss and pray over this sensitive issue that is very likely to touch hearts and challenge faith. I can think of nobody better than John to help us address the topics of assisted suicide, euthanasia, the value of every human life and what the Bible teaches us about dying well. He has a true pastor's heart, a deep understanding and love of Scripture and the medical knowledge and experience needed to guide us through these important ethical and personal matters. These qualities come out so well in his introductory DVD talks before each section, and it is also particularly fitting that Philippa Taylor, CARE's bioethics consultant, joins John in these talks.

I believe that *Finishing Line* will bring clarity to the minds, and comfort for the emotions of those who watch the DVD talks and work through the study booklets. These are matters of life and death, and they're inescapable. I am confident that this resource will be a positive resource that many church leaders will wish to use.

Lyndon Bowring
Executive Chairman, CARE

Introduction
John Wyatt

It is never easy to talk about death, particularly about our own mortality and about what the process of dying might involve for us and for our loved ones. It is a subject that raises uneasy questions and anxieties, reminders of our own frailty and vulnerability. But, as Christian believers, we do not need to share in the terrible fears and despair of those in our society who have no hope.

As people who are changed by the Easter message, we know that death is a defeated enemy. And the truth is that dying well need not be all loss – in fact, it can be a time of opportunity and internal growth, even a strange and wonderful adventure.

So what does it mean to die well and to die faithfully as a Christian believer in the complex, challenging and technological world of modern healthcare? Why is there so much pressure for a change in the law to allow medically assisted suicide for terminally ill people, and can suicide ever be a Christian option?

The aim of this series of five discussions about death and dying is to help us discuss with others, ideally in a small group, some of these difficult but important topics from the perspective of the historic biblical faith. There are no easy answers, but dying need not be a totally negative subject. There are spiritual, human and medical resources to support us on this journey. Our prayer is that you will find encouragement as we address these sensitive issues in a compassionate, biblical and informative way.

The workbook is published alongside a Leaders Guide and DVD. Each session starts with a short video talk by me with a brief introduction by Philippa Taylor. There is then a period for group discussion, using the questions, Bible verses and prayer points in the booklet as a framework.

At the end of the booklet is a list of resources for those who want to take things further.

Thank you for going on this journey with me.

John Wyatt

1

Euthanasia and Medically Assisted Suicide – the current scene

---

This session focuses on the public support and political lobbying for a change in the law to allow medically assisted suicide and euthanasia, and we have started to think about why these topics have become so prominent in today's culture.

Q1 What do you think are some of the personal fears and desires which lie behind the support for the legalisation of euthanasia and medically assisted suicide? Do any of these resonate with you?

Q2 Why do you think euthanasia is supported by many journalists and opinion-formers?

Q3 Why do you think that this issue has become so prominent at this point in Western culture and society? What spiritual issues and trends lie at the root of these fears and desires?

Q4 What do you think might be some of the consequences for individuals and also for society if euthanasia and/or medically assisted suicide were to be legalised? In what ways might it affect us, individually and personally?

 **Notes** ---

Bible passages for reflection

Hebrews 2:14,15

'Since therefore the children share in flesh and blood, he himself likewise partook of the same things, that through death he might destroy the one who has the power of death, that is, the devil, and deliver all those who through fear of death were subject to lifelong slavery.'

Hebrews 9:27

'Just as it is appointed for man to die once, and after that comes judgment.'

Ecclesiastes 9:5,6

'For the living know that they will die, but the dead know nothing, and they have no more reward, for the memory of them is forgotten. Their love and their hate and their envy have already perished, and forever they have no more share in all that is done under the sun.'

John 11:25

'Jesus said to her, "I am the resurrection and the life. Whoever believes in me, though he die, yet shall he live, and everyone who lives and believes in me shall never die. Do you believe this?"'

Closing Prayer

Almighty God, we worship You as the Lord of all Life - Creator, Redeemer and the Judge of us all. We pray about general public opinion and for politicians, medical professional and the media to understand the significance and dangers of changing the law to allow medically assisted dying, or any other form of euthanasia. Amen.

Notes --

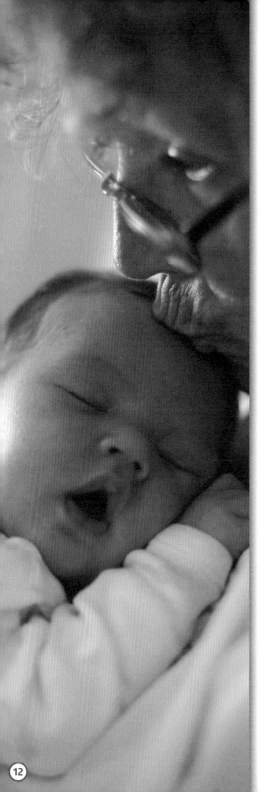

2
What does it mean to be human?

In this session we will be concentrating on the Bible's teaching about what it means to be human. We are created in God's image – as wonderful, special, mysterious and unique beings. But in God's creation plans it seems that we are also designed to be fragile, frail, vulnerable and dependent.

Q1 Why do many Christian believers fear the possibility of dependence or being a burden to others in old age? Why do you think that we find it so hard to accept caring from others? How would you feel if you became dependent on your family or other carers?

Q2 To what extent is dependence part of our creation design as human beings, and to what extent part of our fallenness and our sinful nature? What is the biblical and other evidence in support of this? What positive value might there be in our human fragility, dependence and vulnerability?

Q3 What can we learn about God's plans for human beings from the Incarnation – the God who takes on human flesh and calls us into relationship with himself and with others?

Q4 In what practical ways could our local Christian community be better at mutual caring and burden-sharing? Are there good examples where this is already happening? Are there ways in which I could be more involved?

'...earth to earth, ashes to ashes, dust to dust; in sure and certain hope of the resurrection to eternal life, through our Lord Jesus Christ...'.
Book of Common Prayer

'Dependence is not an alien, subhuman, undignified condition; it is part of the narrative of every human life.'
(from talk)

📝 **Notes** --

Bible passages for reflection

Genesis 1:26-28

'Then God said, "Let us make man in our image, after our likeness. And let them have dominion over the fish of the sea and over the birds of the heavens and over the livestock and over all the earth and over every creeping thing that creeps on the earth." So God created man in his own image, in the image of God he created him; male and female he created them. And God blessed them. And God said to them, "Be fruitful and multiply and fill the earth and subdue it, and have dominion over the fish of the sea and over the birds of the heavens and over every living thing that moves on the earth."'

Genesis 2:7

'…then the LORD God formed the man of dust from the ground and breathed into his nostrils the breath of life, and the man became a living creature.'

Psalm 103:13,14

'As a father shows compassion to his children, so the LORD shows compassion to those who fear him. For he knows our frame; he remembers that we are dust.'

Galatians 6:2

'Bear one another's burdens, and so fulfil the law of Christ.'

'We are dependent beings and to make independence our goal is to fly in the face of reality.'
Gilbert Meilaender

'I am designed to be a burden to you and you are designed to be a burden to me … And the life of a family, including that of the local church, should be one of 'mutual burdensomeness.'"
(from talk)

'If dependence is good enough for Jesus then perhaps it should be good enough for us.'
Anon

'Jesus was with us in the darkness of the womb as he will be with us in the darkness of the tomb.'
Gilbert Meilaender

Philippians 2:5-8

'Have this mind among yourselves, which is yours in Christ Jesus, who, though he was in the form of God, did not count equality with God a thing to be grasped, but emptied himself, by taking the form of a servant, being born in the likeness of men. And being found in human form, he humbled himself by becoming obedient to the point of death, even death on a cross.'

 Closing Prayer

Loving Father, we depend on You for everything! Thank You that Christ lived among us, sharing our human frailty and even dying on the cross. You care so much for those who are weak and suffering. Send us out to support others with the skill and compassion You give. Amen.

Notes ---

3

Can suicide ever be a Christian way to die?

In this session we focus on the painful and disturbing topic of suicide. Some prominent voices are arguing that it can be an act of Christian compassion to help a terminally ill person kill themselves. But both the Bible and 2,000 years of Church teaching are opposed to suicide, seeing it not as a noble and responsible way to die, but as an act of despair and hopelessness.

Q1 What are some of the reasons you think could drive people to suicide? Why do you think that suicide is never celebrated in the Scriptures or in Christian history as a noble and godly way to die?

Q2 How does suicide affect loved ones, relatives and friends?

Q3 Do you think it could ever be an act of compassion to help someone kill themselves, if they are desperate to die?

'Love is a way of saying to a person it's good that you are alive, it's good that you are in the world'
Joseph Pieper

Q4 Is there a difference between suicide and martyrdom? If so, what is the difference?

Q5 How would you respond practically if a close friend or relative expressed suicidal thoughts or was at risk of suicide? What more do you think that churches or Christian communities could do to support those with suicidal thoughts?

'Suicide is to throw your life away because there is nothing worth living for, it is an act of despair; martyrdom is to give your life because there is something even more wonderful to die for, it is an act of faith and hope' (Anon)

Notes --

Bible passages for reflection

1 Corinthians 3:16,17

'Do you not know that you are God's temple and that God's Spirit dwells in you? If anyone destroys God's temple, God will destroy him. For God's temple is holy, and you are that temple.'

1 Corinthians 6:19,20

'Or do you not know that your body is a temple of the Holy Spirit within you, whom you have from God? You are not your own, for you were bought with a price. So glorify God in your body.'

Jeremiah 29:11

'"For I know the plans I have for you," declares the Lord, "plans for welfare and not for evil, to give you a future and a hope."'

John 10:10

'The thief comes only to steal and kill and destroy. I came that they may have life and have it abundantly.'

Matthew 27:3-5

'Then when Judas, his betrayer, saw that Jesus was condemned, he changed his mind and brought back the thirty pieces of silver to the chief priests and the elders, saying, "I have sinned by betraying innocent blood." They said, "What is that to us? See to it yourself." And throwing down the pieces of silver into the temple, he departed, and he went and hanged himself.'

'Suicide ... expresses a desire to be free but not also finite, a desire to be more like Creator than creature. .'
Gilbert Meilaender

🙌 Closing Prayer

Lord of all compassion, please draw near to anyone who is in such despair and pain that they are considering suicide. Grant wisdom and understanding to their families and friends, and to doctors, counsellors and others seeking to help them in this dark night of the soul. Please comfort those mourning for loved ones who have ended their lives. Amen.

📝 Notes ---

4

Dying well and dying faithfully – personal aspects

Today's session provides an opportunity for us to reflect on what it means to die well and to die in a manner consistent with the Christian faith. Dying need not be a totally negative experience. As many who have gone before us have found, the end of our lives on this earth may be transformed by God's grace into an opportunity for growth and internal healing.

Q1 Can you think of any personal examples of a Christian believer who died well? What can we learn from their example? How is this different from a difficult or negative experience of death?

Q2 Do you think it is true that dying well can offer opportunities for blessing and healing? If so what are those opportunities – for the dying person, for those around them, and for the local church?

Q3 Why do you think that people find it difficult to talk about how they would wish to die? What can we do to encourage more discussion about this topic within churches and with our family and loved ones?

'...One short sleep past, we wake eternally And death shall be no more; Death, thou shalt die.'
John Donne

'Suffering is not a question that demands an answer, it's not a problem that demands a solution, it's a mystery that demands a presence' (Anon)

Bible passages for reflection

Hebrews 12:1,2

'Since we are surrounded by so great a cloud of witnesses, let us also lay aside every weight, and sin which clings so closely, and let us run with endurance the race that is set before us, looking to Jesus, the founder and perfecter of our faith, who for the joy that was set before him endured the cross, despising the shame, and is seated at the right hand of the throne of God.'

Psalm 23:6

'Even though I walk through the valley of the shadow of death, I will fear no evil, for you are with me; your rod and your staff, they comfort me.'

John 11:25,26

'Jesus said to her, "I am the resurrection and the life. Whoever believes in me, though he die, yet shall he live, and everyone who lives and believes in me shall never die. Do you believe this?"'

 Notes

The words of a dying person are important and should be treated with respect, especially if there is communication near the end. It is also important to remember that, when someone is dying, the sense of hearing may be retained long after other senses have gone. The person who appears to be unconscious and in a deep coma could still be able to hear, although they may be unable to respond physically. It is always important to talk to the person with sensitivity and caring, even though there appears to be no response. Here are some words and phrases that might be helpful:

'I love you'
Many of us find it hard to verbalise our deepest thoughts and feelings, but now is an opportunity for sharing from the heart.

'I am praying for you'
Many people at the end of life find it difficult to pray for themselves and assurance of prayers from others brings comfort.

'Thank you for...'

'Please forgive me for...'
Here is an opportunity for reconciliation and restoration of relationships that have become distorted and hurt.

'I forgive you'

'I will walk this road with you to the end.'
The greatest fear is often that of being abandoned and left alone as death approaches.

'We will meet again'
This is a reminder of the Christian hope – it is not the end of the story.

 ## Closing Prayer

Jesus, our risen Saviour and faithful Friend, we are so grateful for the assurance that You will never forsake us and have gone ahead to prepare us a place in Heaven. Thank You for the remembrance of those we know who have died in the faith. Please comfort those nearing the end of their lives and grant them Your peace and confidence in Your promises. Amen.

Notes ----------------

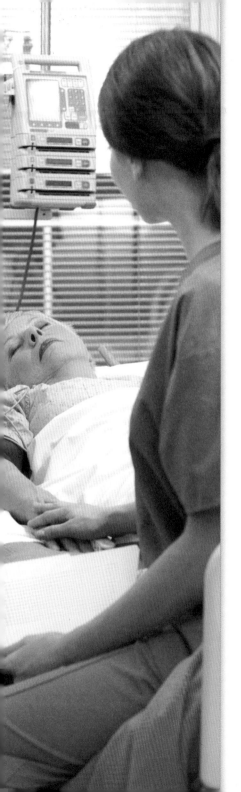

5

Dying well and dying faithfully – medical and legal aspects

In today's discussion, the last one in the series, we continue the theme of what it means to die well and die faithfully – looking particularly at some medical and legal issues. There is evidence that some Christian believers insist on having every possible medical treatment right up to the moment of death – even if the treatment can bring no benefit. Why is this? Christian thinking about death always has a strange ambivalence. Death is not to be welcomed or hastened. Death is an evil, it is described as the last enemy. But although death is an enemy it can by God's grace turn into 'a severe mercy', even a strange form of healing, a gateway to the new heaven and new earth.

Q1 Why do you think that some Christian believers insist on every possible medical treatment right up to the very end of life? What do you think are some of the reasons why it might be difficult sometimes to say 'enough is enough'? Can you think of any biblical material that would be relevant and helpful for this dilemma?

Q2 How can we know when 'enough is enough' and that treatment should stop?

'You matter because you are you, and you matter to the end of your life. Not only will we help you die with dignity but we will help you to live before you die.'
Cicely Saunders

📝 **Notes** --

The next three questions deal with specific personal details about how we would like to die. Of course they are not easy questions to answer, but it is helpful for all of us to start reflecting on these issues.

Q3 How and where would you most prefer to die? Who would you ideally wish to be there with you? What treatments (if any) would you like to continue?

Q4 If on medication, would you like to be able to communicate with your loved ones and carers or would you prefer to be drowsy and sleepy as the end approaches?

Q5 What would you like to communicate to the medical team and other carers in the last days about your care, treatment and decision-making, if you were unable to communicate in person?

'You don't have to kill the patient in order to kill the pain.'
Cicely Saunders

'Hope is to hear the melody of the future: Faith is to dance to that melody in the present.'
Anon

Bible passages for reflection

2 Timothy 4:6-8

'For I am already being poured out as a drink offering, and the time of my departure has come. I have fought the good fight, I have finished the race, I have kept the faith. Henceforth there is laid up for me the crown of righteousness, which the Lord, the righteous judge, will award to me on that day, and not only to me but also to all who have loved his appearing.'

Philippians 1: 21-23

'For to me, to live is Christ and to die is gain. But if I am to live on in the flesh, this will mean fruitful labour for me; and I do not know which to choose. But I am hard-pressed from both directions, having the desire to depart and be with Christ, for that is very much better…'

Job 19:25-27

'For I know that my Redeemer lives, and at the last he will stand upon the earth.

And after my skin has been thus destroyed, yet in my flesh I shall see God,

whom I shall see for myself, and my eyes shall behold, and not another.

My heart faints within me!'

1 Corinthians 15:42-44

'So is it with the resurrection of the dead. What is sown is perishable; what is raised is imperishable. It is sown in dishonour; it is raised in glory. It is sown in weakness; it is raised in power. It is sown a natural body; it is raised a spiritual body.'

 Closing Prayer

God of all hope, please give us wisdom and courage to think about the 'finishing line' of our own lives. Thank You for every provision of care, palliative treatments and other support available to us and those close to us. I trust You, Lord, that at the end You will be our comforting and peaceful presence. Amen

Notes ----------------

Resources for further reading and support

Official Government information on lasting power of attorney
www.gov.uk/power-of-attorney/overview

NHS information on advance decision to refuse treatment
www.nhs.uk/Planners/end-of-life-care/Pages/advance-decision-to-refuse-treatment.aspx

National Council for Palliative Care - the umbrella charity for all those involved in palliative, end of life and hospice care in England, Wales and Northern Ireland.
www.ncpc.org.uk

Dying Matters – a secular organisation which aims to help people talk more openly about dying, death and bereavement, and to make plans for the end of life.
www.dyingmatters.org/overview/about-us

Books

Matters of Life and Death, John Wyatt, InterVarsity Press

The Art of Dying, Living Fully into the Life to Come, Rob Moll, InterVarsity Press

Living Well and Dying Faithfully: Christian Practices for End-of-Life Care, John Swinton, Eerdmans

Facing serious illness
Christian Medical Fellowship

The Human Journey, Peter Saunders, Christian Medical Fellowship

Live and Let Live, Peter Saunders, CARE booklet and online

What to do when someone dies, CARE online

Code Red, Andrew Drain, Christian Medical Fellowship

Tracing the Rainbow - Walking Through Loss and Bereavement, Pablo Martinez, IVP

Right to Die , John Wyatt, InterVarsity Press (in press)

Organisations

CARE
www.care.org.uk

Christian Medical Fellowship
www.cmf.org.uk

Care Not Killing
www.carenotkilling.org.uk

Notes --